WAYS

OF

HEALING

LISA KELLY

All Scripture references are from the New International Version of the
Bible published prior to 2011, unless otherwise indicated.

When referring to the Lord, the pronoun "He" is capitalized, to place
special emphasis on the Lord.
Conversely when referring to the enemy, his name is not capitalized
intentionally.

ACKNOWLEDGEMENTS

I want to thank three special friends from Oklahoma who have helped me publish this book, Charles Bello, Brian Blount, and Jeanine Blount.

Thank you Brian for designing the beautiful book cover and for driving the publishing process for me. Your help has been greatly appreciated.

Thank you Jeanine for the hours you spent uploading and formatting the book for publication.

Charles, thank you for reading this manuscript, encouraging me and giving me helpful feedback. Your suggestions helped to make this a better book.

Table of Contents

INTRODUCTION

Over the years my husband Brad and I have worked closely with an indigenous church-planting ministry in India called Covenant Churches. The ministry is led by James and Sarah Rebbavarapu. Many years ago we formed a 501c3 charity in the United States to help raise funds for the work in India. We are starting to slow down a bit now, but for the past 20 years Brad and I would travel to India once or twice a year for ministry purposes. We also give personally to support the pastors and missionaries who carry the burden of the work day in and day out.

The ministry in India has trained 2,300 pastors, who oversee 7,000 churches. The ministry cares for many orphans and disabled children in family style residential homes. Hundreds of disadvantaged children are given a good education, and a hot meal daily so that they might be able to escape the cycle of poverty.

The ministry is located in the states of Andhra Pradesh and Telangana, and it is predominantly a work among the poorest of the poor, such as Dalits and tribal people. Our heart is to bring healing and wholeness to as many people as possible through our initiatives and through the healing power of Christ. First and foremost the good news of Jesus Christ is preached to the people. This message brings hope to many and breaks the power of hopelessness. Without this hope in Christ, the poor are locked into a religious and cultural system from which

1

they can never escape, even in death. Through Christ their circumstances can and do change for the better.

Healing has been a hallmark of this move of God in India. Over the years the ministry has seen thousands of people healed and saved by the grace of God. Oftentimes when our pastors pray for unbelievers and they are healed, the person gives their life to Christ. Their family witnesses the miracle of healing in their loved one, and they too want to know Jesus and become believers. It's a wonderful thing to see an entire family receive salvation.

Here is a testimony from one of our Covenant pastors to illustrate this point, and maybe it will increase your faith for your own family to know Christ one day. "Pastor K went to visit a certain area and he met two sisters. He shared the gospel with them and they became Christians. The next day one sister's husband, "G", came home drunk and fell asleep on a bench in front of their house. He fell off the bench and became paralyzed. Pastor K visited the family and told them not to lose faith. He said that if they believed, they would see the glory of God. Pastor K prayed for "G" and he was able to lift his arm a little. Pastor K returned the next day and anointed his body with oil, and "G" was completely healed. The whole family now believes in Jesus."

Our pastors experience this fairly often. People in India are aware of the reality of spiritual powers. They will seek healing from their various gods and witch doctors, etc. usually to no avail. When they see the real thing, they recognize it and they are drawn to it.

A number of our Covenant churches were launched through God's healing power. This happens when someone in a village is suffering from an incurable disease or is known to be near death, and nothing has worked to cure the person. When he or she is healed suddenly through the mighty power of Christ, everyone in the village notices that something has happened. They witness the healing power of God in their midst and they want to know more. They want to experience this themselves.

Pastor T shared a story about "P", a 25 year-old man. "P" works in a shop that uses acid, and one day he went to work and accidentally (or intentionally?) swallowed some acid. He burned his whole digestive tract and wasn't able to eat anything. After 40 days, doctors weren't able to offer him any hope, and sent him home to die. When Pastor T was visiting the area, people learned that he was a pastor and told him about "P's" dire situation. Pastor "T" shared the gospel with him, and anointed him with oil and prayed for his healing.

"P" was healed on the spot. Everyone there was astonished. Pastor T told them that he would come back again the following week. The people were happy about this. When he returned, he brought with him with a sound system and mats for people to sit on. People gathered and a new congregation was born." Would this new church have started without "P's" healing taking place? Perhaps. This one miraculous healing raised everyone's faith level that this could happen for them. They wanted to know more about this one true God who cared about the suffering of others.

3

Millions of people in India live in extreme poverty. Many live in small huts, which have no running water or toilets. Many of the poor don't have enough food to eat on a daily basis. When they are sick, medical care is geographically far away, and financially out of reach for many. Every day life is a challenge for survival. If you have never been to India it might be hard for you to grasp just how hard life there is for so many.

We have visited many villages and prayed for many people. Many of the villagers labor in the fields. They carry large heavy bundles on their shoulders. The women walk long distances to the river to get their water each day and carry the water in large jugs on their head. Is it any wonder that their backs ache constantly, or their heads hurt? Knees and shoulders too. As we pray for them, Jesus has mercy on them and heals their aches and pains. No illness is too big or too small for Jesus to heal.

I remember the day God deeply touched my heart for India. Brad had just returned from his first trip to India. Our pastor in Tulsa asked him to share about the trip on Sunday morning. Brad told a story about a village he and our son had visited. It was one of the ministry's earliest church plants.

Many paid assassins lived in this village. The wives of some of the assassins would go to the Covenant church on Sunday, and return home after the service. When they got home their husbands beat them, because they had gone to church. Despite the beatings and the persecution, the women continued to go to church each week.

One day their husbands got tired of beating them. After a time the husbands began to see something different about their wives and they were curious about this. Some of the men began coming to church with their wives, and over time many gave their lives to Christ. A remarkable transformation has taken place in this village.

As I listened to this story, I was greatly moved by it and by the courage of the women. That day my heart was broken for the women of India and the suffering they endure. Over a period of eighteen years, I have taken teams of women to do conferences for our pastor's wives and leaders. We pray for them and encourage them, and teach them basic things about Christianity that most of us know, but they don't have access to. Many don't read or write. We teach them how much God loves them and cares for them in every aspect of their lives, including healing their bodies and emotional pains.

The Indian women's faith is so simple and so strong. During our conferences hundreds of women are healed of all sorts of conditions. We tell them that God desires to heal them and they believe it. We set the captives free and release the oppressed. We lay hands on every woman who attends, and we pray for them and anoint them with oil, and ask the Holy Spirit to heal them. It is a beautiful thing to behold when the God of the universe touches these women and heals them.

When one sees God's compassion for the downtrodden, it helps us to know that what is revealed in the New

Testament is still true for today and true for each one of us. Seeing and experiencing these things with my own eyes has helped me to increase my faith for healing for others as well as for myself. Because of my many experiences with the Lord in healing, and the many promises contained in Scripture, I am convinced that God's love and compassion for us is so great that we can all receive his healing touch whenever we need it.

When it comes to healing many of us give us up too soon. We give up sometimes because we aren't sure whether God wants to heal us personally or we don't know what other options we might have available to us. I want to encourage you to never give up on God.

There is an old saying I was taught as a child: "If at first you don't succeed, try, try again." Our parents taught us this saying, so that we would persevere in the face of failure. We were to keep trying until we succeeded, until we broke through. This principle can be applied to healing. If we don't give up, i.e. if we keep pursuing healing, it will be ours.

My hope is that as you read about the many different ways God has healed people in the past, and the ways He continues to heal today, you will be encouraged that God wants to give you the healing you so desperately desire. God's love and mercy are so great that He doesn't want any of us to suffer with illness or physical pain. Through Christ, our heavenly Father has made a way for us to come into the fullness of his wonderful Kingdom and all that it represents.

HEALING PLUS FORGIVENESS OF SIN

CHAPTER ONE

"Praise the LORD, O my soul, and forget not all his benefits-- **who forgives all your sins and heals all your diseases,** who redeems your life from the pit and crowns you with love and compassion, who satisfies your desires with good things." (Psalm 103)

The Lord forgives all of our sins and He heals all of our diseases. I am linking these two aspects of God's loving nature here for a reason. This is because healing belongs to all believers as much as forgiveness of sins does.

When we first become Christians, we are told that we have received many wonderful things from the Lord, and this is true. Our sins are forgiven and our relationship with God has been restored. We have been given the gift of eternal life and when it is our time to die, we will go to heaven and be with the Lord forever. We are also given the right to become sons and daughters of the living God. We are heirs with Christ. And so much more.

All of these wonderful promises are in the Bible and are some of the foundation stones of our faith. Most of us easily accept these scriptural promises to be true. We believe God for these things. But, somehow, when it comes to believing God's promises for us concerning healing, some of us struggle. Why is this? These promises are all one and the same, meaning they all belong to us.

The promises concerning healing are just as much ours as the promises relating to eternal life and forgiveness of sin.

Healing belongs to us as much as forgiveness of sins
Jesus was pierced, He was crushed for us, not just that we might be free of sin, and the curse of sin and death, but that we might also be set free from sickness. Isaiah says that Jesus bore our sicknesses and carried our diseases, and that by his wounds we are healed. "Surely He took up our infirmities (sicknesses) and carried our sorrows (diseases), yet we considered him stricken by God, smitten by him, and afflicted. But He was pierced for our transgressions, He was crushed for our iniquities; the punishment that brought us peace was upon him, and by his wounds we are healed." (Isaiah 53:4,5)

Isaiah was given this prophetic word about the coming Savior some 700 years before the birth of Christ. God's plan included healing as well as forgiveness of sins and reconciliation with him. "He took up our sicknesses and carried our diseases." The Lord did this so that we might be free from sickness in the same way we can free from sin.

Let me give you a further confirmation about the meaning of the above verses in Isaiah. The gospel writer, Matthew, tells us that many were set free from spirits and demon possession and healed of their sicknesses and that this was a fulfillment of what the prophet Isaiah spoke so long ago. Here is the passage: "When evening came, many who were demon-possessed were brought to him, and He drove out the spirits with a word and healed all the sick. This was to fulfill what was spoken through the prophet Isaiah: "He took up our infirmities and carried our diseases." (Matt.8:16,17)

The disciples who walked with Jesus 2,000 years ago, made this connection. They understood that the miracles and the healings they were seeing and experiencing was a direct fulfillment of the prophecy given by Isaiah so many years before.

Healing was Accepted in Jesus' Day

Healing seemed to be more accepted in Jesus' day than it is today. Let me explain why I believe this to be true. God gave me an interesting insight on this some time ago. I was reading the story of the paralytic, which is found in Luke 5:17-26. Jesus was teaching a crowd of people, and there were some Pharisees and teachers of the law there. The passage says that the power of the Lord was present for him to heal the sick. This means that some healing must have been taking place in the meeting.

A paralyzed man was brought into the meeting by his friends so that Jesus could pray for him to be healed. Jesus didn't immediately heal the man, but first told him that his sins were forgiven. The Pharisees and teachers of the law had an interesting reaction to this. They were upset because Jesus forgave the man's sins. Jesus goes on to heal the paralyzed man and He said this: "that you may know that the Son of Man has authority on earth to forgive sins." Jesus healed the man of his paralysis so that everyone would know that He was also able to forgive sins. Jesus' ability to forgive the sins of others was a new concept to the religious leaders (and probably to everyone else in the room too), and the religious leaders thought that Jesus was blaspheming. They found this idea very hard to accept.

How different it is today in the Western church! Many of us easily believe in Jesus' ability to forgive our sins, but we sometimes aren't as sure about his ability or willingness to heal us. Meanwhile in the Jewish church 2,000 years ago, the religious leaders were relatively ok with healing, but weren't as happy about Jesus saying He forgave the sins of the paralyzed man.

Jesus desires to heal believers today just as much as He desires to forgive our sins. He doesn't limit us and only forgive some of our sins, but rather He forgives ALL of our sins. It is the same with the healing Jesus offers us. He doesn't limit us and only heal some of our sickness and pain, but He heals ALL of our diseases.

Other Issues

Now those religious leaders had lots of other issues with Jesus, like when He healed someone on the Sabbath or in the temple area. Note that their problem concerned when and where Jesus healed, not the fact that He healed. I found one of their statements interesting in light of what I've been sharing here: "Indignant because Jesus had healed on the Sabbath, the synagogue ruler said to the people, "There are six days for work. So come and be healed on those days, not on the Sabbath." Luke 13:14.

There were other things the religious leaders didn't like about what Jesus was doing, but most of those things had to do with Jesus not following their rules and traditions. Things such as Jesus eating with tax collectors and sinners; Jesus driving out demons, they didn't understand it; Jesus' disciples not washing their hands before they ate; and Jesus' disciples eating and drinking and not fasting and praying like they did. (Mt.9:11; Mt.9:34: Mt. 15:1-2; Lk.5:33)

Healing was Commonplace

Jesus healed everywhere He went. It was part of who He was and what He did. All the disciples, the teachers of the law, and the people themselves accepted the fact that Jesus was there to heal the sick. And the Luke passage above goes on to tell us: "Everyone was amazed and gave praise to God. They were filled with awe and said "We have seen remarkable things today." The peoples' reaction to the healing works of Jesus was one of awe and amazement. (Mt.9:33;13:54;15:31; Mark 1:27;5:20; 6:2)

Have you ever wondered why Paul and Peter didn't write more about healing in their letters to various churches? I believe it is because divine healing was taking place in their midst all the time. It was so commonplace that they didn't have to teach on it. Jesus first modeled it, then He sent out his 12 apostles and 72 disciples to heal the sick and preach the kingdom of God. Before Jesus went to the cross, there were 84 other people in Jerusalem and Israel healing the sick and preaching the good news of the kingdom. After Jesus' death and resurrection, and following Pentecost, there were likely even more disciples healing the sick.

Paul and Peter don't write about the kingdom of God as much either for the same reason. It was being preached all the time. That was part of their mandate from Jesus: "Heal the sick who are there and tell them, the kingdom of God is near you." (Luke 10:9) Therefore, the Apostles' time was often spent addressing other issues the believers were facing, such as persecution, baptism, marriage, communion, unity among believers and so on.

The Lord is our Healer

First and foremost the Lord himself is the Healer of our bodies, our minds, our spirits, our thoughts and our emotions. Doctors and medicines are a wonderful provision from the Lord, but they are not meant to be a substitute in place of the Lord's power and presence working in us. Doctors and medicines are to be a help to us while we are pursuing our healing with the Lord and waiting for it to be manifested in our bodies by faith, and not a replacement for divine healing.

The Apostle Paul tells us that we are to offer up our bodies as living sacrifices to the Lord as a spiritual act of worship on our parts. (Romans 12:1) He says that this is holy and pleasing to the Lord. This means that we are to think of our bodies as belonging to the Lord, and are to be careful how we use our bodies. We want to give the Lord dominion over our bodies as an act of our will, in the same way that we give the Lord our souls/spirits when we are born again. Many of us don't think to do this, or don't realize that we are to do this. Everything in our lives works so much better when we place it into the hands of our loving heavenly Father, and that includes our bodies.

King Asa

We don't want to be like King Asa was near the end of his life. Asa was King over Judah and did much to please the Lord during the course of his life. He and the people of Judah had given themselves wholeheartedly to the Lord and had seen the Lord's power defeat their enemies in a mighty way.

Then something changed. Towards the end of Asa's life, his heart seemed to harden. Instead of looking to the Lord for help when an enemy attacked them, he looked to another king, the king of Aram, for help. And he brutally oppressed some of his people.

Then near the end of his reign, Asa was afflicted with a really bad disease in his feet. "In the thirty-ninth year of his reign Asa was afflicted with a disease in his feet. Though his disease was severe, even in his illness he did not seek help from the LORD, but only from the physicians." (2 Chronicles 16:12) Asa was really sick and didn't ask the Lord to help him. He placed more trust in his doctors than he did in the Lord. He died two years later from this disease.

Doctors VS Divine Healing

How many of us sometimes don't seek help from the Lord for our illnesses? Some of us don't even know we can do this. But others of us have experienced the Lord's healing

13

at times, and yet we find ourselves in this situation. We forget to seek his help, or we choose not to for some reason.

It's time for us to change our thought processes regarding healing. We want to train ourselves to turn to God first and to doctors second. Many of us have this backwards. We go to the doctor first, and when that doesn't work, we go to the Lord.

Jesus is our Healer and He loves us so much. Why wouldn't we want to go to him right away with any problems we might be having? As we do this, the Lord will lead us to our next step. It is very possible that the Lord will lead us to go to our doctor for treatment. Or He may heal us suddenly in a supernatural way, or heal us using other means.

Doctors and medicines are a wonderful provision from the Lord. It was God who created these skills and medicines in order to help mankind, and to help his beloved children. It is perfectly ok to go to your doctor and take medicines, while you are praying and pressing in to the Lord for your healing, while you are waiting for the Lord to act on your behalf. You don't want to ignore potentially dangerous medical conditions. It is wise to keep any illnesses or diseases under good control until healing comes.

God is interested in everything that pertains to us, just as we are interested in our own children. Nothing is too small to bring to his attention. Never feel like you are bothering the Lord with your problems. He is the one who has all the answers for us.

CHAPTER TWO

When it comes to the subject of healing, we can all have some faulty thinking at times because of our experiences with healing or our lack of them. Any kind of wrong thinking about healing can inhibit our ability to seek after and receive healing from the Lord's hand. Some examples might be:

- If God wanted me to be healed, He would have done it by now.
- If it is his will that I be healed, why did He allow me to get sick in the first place? Therefore, healing must not be his will.
- I know God heals some people, but does He want to heal me specifically?
- God has allowed me to be sick because He wants to refine me in some way.
- God has called me to a higher level of suffering for him.
- God is using me in an effective way, so I have to put up with the sickness the enemy afflicts me with.
- I have to walk this sickness out while I wait for the Lord to deliver me.
- God doesn't love me or care about me. If He did, He wouldn't have allowed this to happen.
- It's my own fault. I wouldn't be sick if I hadn't done such and such.
- I deserve this sickness because of my past sins. God is punishing me.
- I caused this pain when I worked so hard all week; now I have to live with it.

17

If we are honest with ourselves, haven't we all had some of these sorts of thoughts when our healing was delayed? It would be good for us to ask the Holy Spirit to show us if any kind of wrong thinking has crept in regarding healing, so that our thought processes don't get in the way of our healing. Doubt and unbelief are the opposite of faith, and sometimes this is operating in us without our even knowing it.

Healing is part of our inheritance in Christ. Because there has been some confusion on the subject of healing, I felt it would be helpful to lay out some additional arguments in favor of healing, in order to increase your faith in God's desire to heal and in his willingness to heal each one of us.

Jesus came to heal the sick and set the captives free. In Luke 4 Jesus goes to Nazareth, and stands up in the synagogue. He reads from the scroll of Isaiah 61. "The Spirit of the Lord is on me, because He has anointed me to preach good news to the poor. He has sent me to proclaim freedom for the prisoners and recovery of sight for the blind, to release the oppressed, to proclaim the year of the Lord's favor." After Jesus read the passage, He then said: "Today this scripture is fulfilled in your hearing."

Jesus announced that God's Spirit was upon him in order to proclaim freedom for prisoners, recovery of sight for the blind, and to release the oppressed. Part of Jesus' mission is to set the captives free and to undo the works of the enemy. Sickness and disease are some of the works of the enemy. The enemy is the one who steals, kills and destroys, while Jesus came that we may have life, and have it abundantly. (John 10:10)

Jesus proclaimed that today this scripture was now fulfilled. That was more than 2,000 years ago, and it is as true today as it was when Jesus first announced it. How do I know this? Because Jesus is the same person today that He was 2,000 years ago. The word tells us this. It says "Jesus Christ is the same yesterday and today and forever." (Heb.13:8) What He was yesterday, He is today and will be tomorrow. We can count on that. Jesus was healing multitudes 2,000 years ago; He is healing us today; and He will still be healing us, and others tomorrow. We are living in the time of his favor.

Jesus healed ALL who came to him.

Jesus desired to heal all of the people who came to him, and there are recorded instances of this happening in the gospels. Matthew 8:16 tells us "When evening came, many who were demon-possessed were brought to him, and He drove out the spirits with a word and **healed all the sick**. Some other passages illustrating this are: Luke 6:19; Luke 4:41; Matt. 12:15; Matt. 9:35; and Mark 6:56.

There are only a few recorded exceptions to this premise, such as when Jesus went back to his hometown of Nazareth. He was only able to do a few miracles there because of the unbelief of the people. The Nazarenes knew Jesus as the son of Joseph and Mary, and they couldn't get over that barrier to see who He really was. Unbelief and not knowing who God is and what He is like may also prevent us from receiving our healing too. The remedy is simple. We can choose to believe God's word and see things from his viewpoint.

Do we tend to focus on the few in the Bible who weren't healed, or do we place our attention on the multitudes that were healed? One focus builds faith while another diminishes it. To build a theology on what Jesus didn't do, rather than on all He did accomplish is an incomplete viewpoint.

It is the same kind of thinking that lies behind the theory of how we see life: do we see our glass as half full or half empty? If one sees their glass as half empty all the time, one is always dissatisfied with their circumstances. In Christ our glass is always half full, on its way to being completely filled up to overflowing. We aren't to focus on what is missing, but rather on what is possible in Christ. He is the God of the impossible. With him all things are always possible.

Healing is in the heart of the Father and the Son. Jesus came to reveal the Father to us, to show us what He was like. Jesus is the exact representation of the Father. Everything that Jesus said and did was at the bidding of his Father. "The words I say to you are not just my own. Rather, it is the Father, living in me, who is doing his work." Jesus came to do the will of the Father here on earth. (John 14:10; Heb.1:3; John 6:38)

What is the Father's will and work? Looking at Jesus will give us the answer. Jesus moved in compassion for the sick and the lost, the broken and the hungry, the weak and the poor. He raised the dead to life, healed the sick, restored sight to the blind, cast out demons, fed the hungry, restored hurting people back into society, and spoke about the Kingdom of God to multitudes. In all these things Jesus reflected the Father's heart for mankind.

Matthew 4 gives a good description of Jesus' ministry while He walked among us: "Jesus went throughout Galilee, teaching in their synagogues, preaching the good news of the kingdom, and healing every disease and sickness among the people. News about him spread all over Syria, and people brought to him all who were ill with various diseases, those suffering severe pain, the demon-possessed, those having seizures, and the paralyzed, and He healed them." He healed all of those people and He will heal you and me too.

We are under a new and better Covenant than the Israelites were.

The book of Hebrews compares the old covenant under Moses with the new covenant that was established with Jesus as our high priest. We are told that "The ministry Jesus has received is as superior to theirs (old testament covenant under Moses) as the covenant of which He is mediator is superior to the old one, and it is founded on better promises." (Heb. 8:6) The new covenant we have as Christians is superior to the old one under Moses, and it is founded on better promises.

Many of us may not realize that under the old covenant

21

of Moses God provided a way for the Israelites to be free from sickness and disease. The Lord revealed himself to the Israelites as Jehovah Rapha. He told them that He was the Lord who healed them. (Ex. 15:26) Healing has been part of God's plan for his people for a very long time.

"If you pay attention to these laws and are careful to follow them, then the LORD your God will keep his covenant of love with you, as He swore to your forefathers. He will love you and bless you and increase your numbers. He will bless the fruit of your womb, the crops of your land--your grain, new wine and oil--the calves of your herds and the lambs of your flocks in the land that He swore to your forefathers to give you. You will be blessed more than any other people; none of your men or women will be childless, nor any of your livestock without young. The LORD will keep you free from every disease. He will not inflict on you the horrible diseases you knew in Egypt, but he will inflict them on all who hate you." (Deut.7:12-15)

"Worship the LORD your God, and his blessing will be on your food and water. I will take away sickness from among you, and none will miscarry or be barren in your land. I will give you a full life span." (Exodus 23:25-26)

If the Israelites followed the instructions of the Lord, they didn't have to worry about sickness. Not only would the Lord heal the Israelites, but He would also prevent them from getting sick in the first place. Under a covenant far inferior to ours, the children of Israel had the potential of going through life without sickness or disease, and with the ability to live a full life span.

Under the new covenant, we are given the right to become children of God. Under the old covenant, the Israelites were God's chosen people, his servants, and not his beloved children like we are. If God didn't want the Israelites to be sick, how much more would He not want his sons and daughters to be sick!

Jesus taught his disciples to do what He did.

Jesus wanted his ministry of healing and preaching the good news to continue after his death and He made preparations to see that this would happen. He spent three years with his disciples teaching them and training them how to pray for the sick and cast out demons. Jesus commissioned his disciples to go and do the same things He had been doing.

When Jesus sent out the twelve apostles we are told He "gave them power and authority to drive out all demons and to cure diseases". And He "sent them out to preach the kingdom of God and to heal the sick". (Luke 9:1,2) Healing the sick was surely part of their commissioning by Jesus.

A short while later Jesus commissioned 72 other disciples. Part of their instructions included this: "Heal the sick who are there." (Luke 10:9) I want to highlight that the verses say we are to heal the sick, not pray for the sick and hope for the best, but heal the sick. This was pretty clear wording that Jesus used. Heal the sick.

There was no doubt on the part of Jesus that the 72 and the 12 would not have been able to carry out his instructions to "heal the sick". Jesus had already modeled it for them, and He watched them doing it before He sent them out. They went out and did this in his authority. As disciples and believers, we too can walk in this same authority and anointing.

The book of Acts confirms that the apostles and disciples continued praying for the sick after Jesus had ascended into heaven. "The apostles performed many miraculous signs and wonders among the people." And "Crowds gathered also from the towns around Jerusalem, bringing their sick and those tormented by evil spirits, and all of them were healed." (Acts 5:12; 5:16)

All believers are commissioned by the Lord to do the same works He did. And Jesus told us we would do even greater works than He did because He would be going to the Father. "I tell you the truth, anyone who has faith in me will do what I have been doing. He will do even greater things than these, because I am going to the Father."(John 14:12) So, not only is healing available for us personally, but we are also to be bearers of healing for others.

Think about it for a minute. If Jesus didn't want to continue to heal people after his death, He wouldn't have spent the time and energy training others to do this, would He? And He wouldn't have instructed us to continue to do the things He had been doing. Let this be the day you put aside any doubts you might have about God's willingness to heal you, and believe that He is Jehovah Rapha, the God who heals you.

HEALING METHODS IN THE NEW TESTAMENT
PART ONE

CHAPTER THREE

Jesus healed multitudes from a variety of sicknesses using different methods. Scripture tells us that what is recorded in scripture is only a small part of all that Jesus did. The Apostle John stated that if everything Jesus did were written down, then 'even the whole world would not have room for the books that would be written.' (Jn.21:25) The Bible gives us a wonderful picture of the healing ministry of our Lord Jesus Christ, but it is only a partial picture.

The word of God is full of insights into how to pray effectively for healing and for everything else that we might need. In this chapter and the one following, we will look at some of the healing methods used by Jesus and his disciples. Other ways were used to heal the sick as well, for example the prayer of command, and some of these methods will be discussed in greater detail in later chapters.

I. LAYING HANDS ON THE SICK
One of the ways Jesus healed people was to lay hands on them. Luke 4:40 tells us this: "When the sun was setting, the people brought to Jesus all who had various kinds of sickness, and laying his hands on each one, He healed them."

This is probably the most common method of healing used

by Christians today. Jesus commissioned all believers to do this. "He (Jesus) said to them, "Go into all the world and preach the good news to all creation.....And these signs will accompany those who believe: ....they will place their hands on sick people, and they will get well." (Mark 16:15-18) As we lay hands on the sick, we are also praying for them to be healed.

Paul's Blindness

The story of Paul's encounter with the risen Jesus on the road to Damascus is an interesting one in that the Lord used several different methods to bring about Paul's conversion and healing from blindness, including the laying on of hands. Paul's healing was both physical and spiritual. The story is found in Acts 9 & 22. Before Paul became an Apostle, he was a Pharisee who persecuted many of the early believers in Jerusalem. He was travelling to Damascus to find believers and take them as prisoners and bring them back to Jerusalem.

During the trip, a bright light flashed from heaven and Jesus appeared to Paul and spoke to him. Following this encounter Paul was blind for three days. His traveling companions had to lead him into the city. During those three days, he fasted and prayed. The Lord showed him a vision of a man named Ananias coming and laying hands on him to restore his sight.

Meanwhile the Lord spoke to Ananias in a vision as well. In the vision the Lord tells Ananias about Paul and commands him to go and see Paul, and to lay hands on him so that his sight might be restored to him. And the Lord shared other things with him about Paul's destiny so that Ananias could encourage him with these things.

When Ananias entered the house, he placed his hands on Paul. He told him "the Lord—Jesus, who appeared to you on the road as you were coming here—has sent me so that you may see again and be filled with the Holy Spirit." Paul's sight was restored. Paul was also filled with the Holy Spirit and baptized. Two beautiful healings in one divinely orchestrated encounter.

Ananias went in obedience, knowing that Paul would be healed, because he had seen it in a vision, through a prophetic gifting. Most of us lay hands on the sick and pray for them in faith without the certainty of knowing the outcome. We can always rely on the faithfulness of God.

Impartation of the Holy Spirit
We see from this passage that the Holy Spirit was imparted to Paul through the laying on of hands. This is also how Peter and John prayed for the believers in Samaria to receive the Holy Spirit. "When they arrived, they prayed for them that they might receive the Holy Spirit, because the Holy Spirit had not yet come upon any of them...........Then Peter and John placed their hands on them, and they received the Holy Spirit. " (Acts 8) So we see that God uses our hands for both healing and the impartation of the Holy Spirit.

II. ELDERS ANOINTING THE SICK WITH OIL

When Jesus sent out the apostles, "They drove out many demons and anointed many sick people with oil and healed them." (Mk.6:13) Pastors and their wives, and church leaders carry an anointing for the people under their care. They also have a positional authority they can use with their members to help them be set free from enemy activity in their lives. This is because a church member has submitted themselves to their leadership. This authority is similar to what parents carry for their young children.

Pastors and elders also have the ability to lay hands on people to impart gifts to them. In speaking to his disciple Timothy, Paul exhorted him to do this: "Do not neglect your gift, which was given you through a prophetic message when the body of elders laid their hands on you." (1 Tim.4:14). Pastors and church leaders carry more authority and anointing for those in their care than they often realize.

This passage in James tells believers to ask their leaders to pray for them and anoint them with oil when they are sick. "Is any one of you sick? He should call the elders of the church to pray over him and anoint him with oil in the name of the Lord. And the prayer offered in faith will make the sick person well; the Lord will raise him up. If he has sinned, he will be forgiven." (James 5:14-15) This is a pretty incredible scripture. The prayer offered in faith will make the sick person well.

If church elders and Pastors would meditate on this

scripture, I believe they would feel more empowered in their prayers for their church members. There is no doubt whatsoever in this passage that the person wouldn't be healed through their prayers and anointing with oil. "The prayer offered in faith will make the sick person well." How clear is that. Our job as a leader is to believe this scripture and pray for those in our care. God's job is to heal the people.

Sometimes we find it hard to ask our leaders for prayer. We don't want to bother them or take up their time. Or maybe we don't ask because we are embarrassed about our condition and don't want anyone to know. Don't let these kinds of thoughts stop you from asking for prayer. The Lord has given us our Pastors and church leaders to guide us, and teach us, but also to pray for us when we are sick. We could begin by asking for prayer from our fellow brothers and sisters in Christ, and if that doesn't bring about the desired result, then the next step might be this one.

III. PREVAILING PRAYER

Power is released when we pray. James 5:16 says: "The prayer of a righteous man is powerful and effective." Prayer is a powerful weapon for all believers. We can apply the power of prayer to our own personal needs or to the needs of others. We can pray and ask God for anything He puts on our heart, and for anything the Bible promises us.

This is prayer we add during the midst of the many trials and difficulties of life. We pray until we have our breakthrough. We pray until the healing is manifested in our bodies and for others. We pray until we have prevailed. A great man of prayer called E.M Bounds once said this about prayer: "Much time spent with God is the secret of all successful praying." God is the answer to everything we need.

There are some healing situations where this type of intercessory prayer is required. In Mark 9 Jesus' disciples tried to cast out a deaf and dumb spirit that was afflicting a boy and they were unable to. When the disciples were alone with Jesus, they asked him why they weren't able to drive out the spirit. Jesus replied "This kind can come out only by prayer." Sometimes prayer and fasting are needed to gain a victory.

Jesus was a man of prayer and He modeled the importance of prayer for us. Luke 5:15,16 tells us that crowds of people were coming to hear Jesus speak and to be healed of their sicknesses. The passage then goes on to say "But Jesus often withdrew to lonely places and prayed." Jesus knew that the only way He could pray effectively for so many people was to spend time with his Father in prayer beforehand. He understood and valued the power of prayer.

Peter Praying

Oftentimes, before we pray for someone who is sick, we will first begin with prayer and then we will lay hands on the person. Acts 9 contains the story of a woman named Tabitha who did many acts of kindness for people in need and she had recently passed away. Her friends asked

Peter to come and this is what he did when he arrived: "Peter sent them all out of the room; then he got down on his knees and prayed. Turning toward the dead woman, he said, "Tabitha, get up." She opened her eyes, and seeing Peter she sat up. He took her by the hand and helped her to her feet. Then he called the believers and the widows and presented her to them alive." Peter used both intercessory prayer and a prayer of command to bring her back to life.

King Hezekiah's Example

King Hezekiah is a great example of someone whose prayer touched the heart of God. Isaiah 38 contains the story. Hezekiah became ill and was at the point of death. The prophet Isaiah went to him and gave him a word from the Lord that he would not recover from this illness. Hezekiah prayed and wept bitterly before the Lord. The Lord then spoke to him through Isaiah and said: "I have heard your prayer and seen your tears; I will add fifteen years to your life. And I will deliver you and this city from the hand of the king of Assyria. I will defend this city." The Lord heard the cry of his heart, and his earnest prayer, and not only extended his life, but promised to deliver Hezekiah and all his people from the hand of the king of Assyria. Prayer is a powerful weapon in a believer's arsenal.

IV. ANOINTED OBJECTS

Sometimes God will allow certain inanimate objects to be used for healing. Objects like clothing or handkerchiefs, or even someone's shadow. How or why this happens I can't say for sure, but my personal feeling is that the anointing, ie the presence of God, on a person can be so strong that it overflows onto other things around him or her. And through prayer this strong anointing has been known to be transferred to objects like prayer cloths. These prayer cloths are sent to sick people. When these anointed cloths are laid on the bodies of the sick, the people are healed.

Jesus' Clothing

Jesus' clothing carried this unique kind of anointing. A woman experienced severe bleeding for 12 years and she continued to get worse. She was desperate, and thought if she could touch the hem of Jesus' garment, she would be healed. When she touched Jesus' cloak, immediately she knew she was completely healed of her affliction. (Mark 5)

The Holy Spirit was so strongly on Jesus that his clothing was infused with all that He carried. Everywhere Jesus went, people wanted to touch the edge of his cloak and all who touched him were healed. "And wherever He went, into villages, towns or countryside, they placed the sick in the market places. They begged him to let them touch even the edge of his cloak, and all who touched him were healed". (Mark 5:56)

Jesus' cloak carried a healing anointing for those who had faith. I say this because the soldiers who took his life, handled his clothing quite a bit and nothing is recorded about any of them being healed. I believe that faith is an important ingredient when obtaining one's healing through anointed objects.

Examples of Others Operating with this Anointing

Apostle Paul: Acts 19 tells us that God did some extraordinary miracles through the apostle Paul. The anointing upon him was so strong that when handkerchiefs and aprons had touched him, and were taken to the sick, "their illnesses were cured and the evil spirits left them."

William Branham: Branham was a powerful evangelist who healed hundreds of thousands of people, if not millions. He would receive thousands of letters from sick people asking him to come and pray for them. It was impossible for him to go to each one, so one day after he read the story in Acts about Paul's handkerchiefs healing people, he felt to take ribbon into his special prayer place. Then he would pray over the ribbon and people's specific illnesses. His helpers would answer each letter and include an anointed ribbon inside. Branham received many reports from people who were healed when they laid the ribbon over their sick body parts.

Smith Wigglesworth: Smith Wigglesworth moved in a healing anointing. One time a distressed woman came to him because her husband's alcoholism was getting very bad. Smith prayed over a piece of cloth and told her to put it under her husband's pillow. She did as instructed, and the next morning her husband had completely lost his taste for alcohol. It tasted like poison to him. When his wife told him what had happened, he was converted on the spot.

A Person's Shadow

God can use a person's shadow to heal another if they have enough faith for healing. A power would be released sometimes when the apostle Peter's shadow would fall on people. The simple act of walking down a street could bring healing to someone if they were in the vicinity of where Peter's shadow happened to fall. This happened often enough that people would position themselves along the streets so that Peter's shadow might fall on them.

"As a result, people brought the sick into the streets and laid them on beds and mats so that at least Peter's shadow might fall on some of them as he passed by. Crowds gathered also from the towns around Jerusalem, bringing their sick and those tormented by evil spirits, and all of them were healed." (Acts 5:15,16) Again, I believe this worked for some people, because they had faith to be healed.

I experienced this one time in my life that I know of. This was some years ago and I was in a meeting where the Lord used me to release joy into the room. My pastor noticed that as I passed by people, they would receive joy without my touching them. He felt it was similar to how Peter's shadow might have touched people.

HEALING METHODS IN THE NEW TESTAMENT
PART TWO

CHAPTER FOUR

In this chapter we will continue laying out some of the various healing methods found in the New Testament.

V. RELEASE OF GOD'S POWER
Every act of healing involves a release of divine power in some way, even though the person receiving healing may or may not feel anything unusual. In this section I want to explain some of the ways God's power can be released unexpectedly in our lives for healing in order to help open the reader up to new possibilities in God.

To put it simply, there are times when the Lord chooses to release his power in ways that surprise us, sovereignly, in individuals and in group settings. Sometimes we can receive healing through a supernatural release of God's power when we aren't even asking God for healing, or when we might not even be aware we are in need of healing. Let me give you some examples to better illustrate what I am saying.

Corporate Flow of Power: Jesus would experience supernatural power flowing from the Holy Spirit, and the power would touch a lot of people at once. Luke 6:17-20 gives us an account of this. Jesus was with a large crowd of his disciples and with a great number of people from all over the area. The people had come to listen to Jesus and to be healed of their diseases. The passage tells us that "those troubled by evil spirits were cured, and the people all tried to touch him, because power was coming from him and healing them all."

What would this look like? To be in a meeting where everyone is healed all at once. I have heard stories of this happening elsewhere but I haven't yet seen it with my own eyes. I believe the same kind of thing was happening in Luke 5:17 when we are told "the power of the Lord was present for him to heal the sick". When we meet together as believers, do we think about the fact that this could happen? Do we ask the Lord to break into our meetings with his mighty flow of power? Knowing it could happen helps to raise our faith levels so that one day we might experience this type of wonderful corporate healing experience.

Kenneth Hagin, a man known for his faith and healing ministry, experienced this happening in one of his meetings. He wrote about it in his little booklet "The Glory of God". He said "he was once in a service where every person in the building was instantly healed and it occurred when the Holy Spirit manifested himself as a wind." He was preaching at a service in Texas when everyone heard the sound of wind blowing through the building. Every person attending the meeting was healed. Isn't this something we would all like to see and experience? It is possible.

There is power when we gather together to pray. Jesus spoke these words: "Again, I tell you that if two of you on earth agree about anything you ask for, it will be done for you by my Father in heaven. For where two or three come together in my name, there am I with them." (Matt.18:19-20) When we gather together Jesus is in our midst. Isn't that a beautiful thought? He said that if we will agree together in prayer about something, it will be done for us.

Power for Individuals: God loves to surprise his children at times and do special things for us, things we don't even know to ask him for. I've had this happen to me from time to time, and when it does, I find myself in awe of God to an even greater degree.

I had a dream some years ago and in the dream I screamed out. I had a knowing that I had been delivered from a spirit that had gained access during childhood. The name was unknown to me previously, and I had no idea how this thing might have been affecting me, nor did I even know it was there. The Lord knew I needed this and surprised me by setting me free as I slept.

I was speaking with a friend a few years ago and she shared a very similar experience. It had just happened to her and she was still in that wonderful state of awe about it. She had not had an experience like this before and didn't even know it was possible. I didn't either until it happened to me. Because of that I wanted to make you aware of this possibility too.

Close to twenty years ago I was attending a conference and the Lord gave me a scripture verse one evening from

Psalm 30:5 "rejoicing comes in the morning". I wondered if the next morning I would receive a gift of joy from the Lord. Morning came and nothing happened. Then in the afternoon I was having lunch with friends when a "suddenly" happened. I received a huge download of joy that lasted intensely for over six months and stayed with me in smaller doses for years after that.

The Lord gave me the most wonderful gift I had ever received. God conceived something in his heart for me, something He knew I would love, and then He supernaturally imparted it to me. I believe that part of what the Lord was doing with me during that time was healing my heart from past hurts. There is a saying that laughter is the best medicine and that is so true.

A biblical example of this is the time Jacob wrestled with God all night, and in the morning God changed his name and blessed him. Jacob saw the Lord God face to face. Jacob was going back to his home after 20 long years away and he would soon be facing the brother whom he had wronged. He was in great fear and distress over this. Then God came to him and was with him all that night, so Jacob wouldn't be alone with all his thoughts and fears. (Gen.32) God wanted to do something special for Jacob that would be burned into his heart forever. That encounter with God would have had a profound effect on him.

When these kinds of things happen to us, all we can say is 'wow'. We often don't even have the words to describe our spiritual encounters or the deep effect they have on us.

VI. CONFESSION/FORGIVENESS

When we are praying for someone to be healed of a sickness or a disease, sometimes we might perceive that there is something blocking the person's healing. The block may be caused by sin in a person's life, either past or present. The remedy for this is to ask for the Lord's forgiveness and cleansing from any effects of the sin. Not only are we to ask for forgiveness from the Lord and others when necessary, but we are also to forgive others who have hurt us or wronged us.

Forgiveness of sins is one of the many blessings we receive through Christ. It is available to all believers, but it is up to us to avail ourselves of it, meaning we come to Jesus and ask to be forgiven. Or we confess our sins to one another. This is an important part of our walk as Christians. It was part of the Lord's Prayer that Jesus taught his disciples. In Matthew 6 Jesus elaborates on this: "Forgive us our debts, as we also have forgiven our debtors. And lead us not into temptation, but deliver us from the evil one. For if you forgive men when they sin against you, your heavenly Father will also forgive you. But if you do not forgive men their sins, your Father will not forgive your sins."

Let's look at two stories in the gospels where sin was a factor in someone's healing. There was a man who had been an invalid for 38 years and after he was healed, Jesus admonished him: "See, you are well again. Stop sinning or something worse may happen to you." (John

5:14). In the story of the healing of the paralytic, before Jesus prayed for the man's healing, He said to him: "Take heart, son; your sins are forgiven." (Matt.9:2) Jesus knew by the Holy Spirit that their physical ailments were a result of sin in their lives, and the sin needed to be forgiven so that healing could take place.

The apostle James tells us to "confess your sins to each other and pray for each other so that you may be healed." (James 5:16) Sometimes we need each other's help to see our sin or to be able to fully forgive someone who caused us pain. As believers we are part of a royal priesthood. It is a privilege for us to administer forgiveness to another, and help them be reconciled with the Lord. Jesus confirmed this when He told his disciples that, if we forgive anyone their sins, they are forgiven. "If you forgive anyone his sins, they are forgiven; if you do not forgive them, they are not forgiven." (Jn.20:23) We have been given an incredible responsibility and a wonderful tool for healing.

I was raised as a Catholic and had been taught that only ordained priests were allowed to perform this function in the church. Maybe you were raised in a similar way. This is not biblical. All who belong to the Lord have been empowered to do this for one another. It is an act of love. To help a brother or sister in Christ be free of their sins is a beautiful experience. It is a wonderful experience when we are on the receiving end of this kind of prayer as well. One can often tangibly feel God's forgiveness.
So, when we pray for someone for healing, or are asking God for healing for ourselves, we want to be aware of

this possibility so we can ask the Holy Spirit to show us if the cause of our problem, or that of another, is sin related. Then, once confession and forgiveness have taken place, healing will occur.

VII. HEALING THROUGH SPIRITUAL GIFTS

1 Corinthians 12 gives a good explanation of spiritual gifts. This is a big topic and I will only be able to touch on it here. Each and every believer is given a manifestation of the Spirit for the common good. We can all operate in spiritual gifts. The Holy Spirit releases these gifts to us as He determines. There are two different aspects to spiritual gifts that I want to highlight here: Moving in a special gift of healing and using one's spiritual gifts to help bring about a healing.

Gift of Healing: Gifts of healing, miraculous powers, and workers of miracles. Each one of us can exercise a gift of healing, meaning that when we pray for others, supernatural healing power flows through us for another's healing. But there is also a special gift of healing that God sometimes imparts to certain people. It is easily recognized because the person operating in the gift will bring about the healing of hundreds and thousands of people under this anointing. It is our Lord Jesus Christ who does the actual healing. He chooses to do it through certain anointed people and through the body of believers.

Gifts of healing are different from the gift of miracles, although many dramatic healings are also miraculous in nature. I was intrigued once when I was reading the life story of William Branham, who had an incredible healing gift. He saw countless people healed and saved through his ministry. Branham had seen God heal so many people that his faith knew no bounds. He began moving in the gift of miracles too. In one meeting Bill prayed for a 16 year old boy who was born blind, and the boy was miraculously able to see for the first time in his life. There was a mighty release of God's power and hundreds of miracles took place. In that atmosphere everything seemed possible. People were throwing away crutches, and coming up out of their wheelchairs. They were getting up from the stretchers they had been carried in on.

Spiritual Gifts Used in Healing: Some of the other spiritual gifts used in healing might be prophecy, distinguishing between spirits, word of wisdom, word of knowledge, tongues and interpretation of tongues, and faith. All believers can operate in these gifts. All of us have been given a measure of these gifts. These gifts do not belong to us. The Holy Spirit releases them to us as needed for the blessing and healing of others.

When I am praying for someone to be healed, I almost always begin by praying quietly in tongues. As I do, my mind is emptied out and my spirit is engaged. In that place I can more easily receive pictures and impressions from the Lord as to how to pray for the person. Pictures and impressions often come as thoughts passing through our mind.

For many years the Lord would only give me one word, like

44

anger, fear, etc. That one word of knowledge was the key needed to unlock the person's healing. The Lord has given me words of knowledge about others during the night in my dreams, and then I would find myself praying for the person the next day and would know just how to pray. The person was also touched by the fact that God was thinking about them when He caused another person to dream about them.

One time I was in a large meeting and the speaker had a word of knowledge about someone who had been in a car accident many years before and suffered a head injury and it was causing some problems now. Just a day or two before this, I had started feeling dizzy at times and I had been praying and asking the Lord what was causing this. When I heard the word of knowledge, I knew it was for me. It was further confirmed to me, when the speaker put his hand up to his head and it was the exact same spot where I was injured in a car accident when I was 17 years old. I was instantly healed of the dizziness I had been feeling.

Isn't God so kind to us? I would never have thought to tie the car accident into the dizziness I was experiencing. God knew and He helped me and healed me. The Lord's heart is filled with love and mercy and compassion for his children. He wants to heal every one of us. Ask the Lord to fill you with his Holy Spirit and to release more spiritual gifts to you, so that you might be a blessing to others and you yourself might be healed. These gifts are so helpful when it comes to healing.

VIII. PRAYING IN THE NAME OF JESUS

When we know and understand who King Jesus is and who He is in us, and we know who we are in him, we can use his name with great authority. Demons fear and cower at the name of Jesus and all that He represents. On several occasions Jesus exhorts his disciples to pray and ask in his name. (Jn. 14:13; 14:14; 15:16; 16:23; 16:24; 16:26) Jesus said things like "You may ask me for anything in my name and I will do it." And "My father will give you whatever you ask in my name."

We are to do everything in the name of Jesus. "And whatever you do, whether in word or deed, do it all in the name of the Lord Jesus, giving thanks to God the Father through him." (Col. 3:17) Isn't this interesting? We have been given such an immense privilege to use the name of our dear Savior, and yet many of us don't even know about this, or if we know, we don't know how to use his name effectively.

When Peter healed a crippled man, he said these words: "In the name of Jesus Christ of Nazareth, walk." When Peter was explaining this miracle to the people he said: "It is Jesus' name and the faith that comes through him that has given this complete healing to him". Then a short time later Peter was brought before the religious leaders and asked about this and he told them that it was by the name of Jesus Christ of Nazareth that this man stands before them healed. The authorities were so upset about this that they ordered Peter and John not to speak in the name of Jesus. The authorities wouldn't have bothered doing this unless they were afraid of the name of Jesus. (Acts 3:6; 3:16; 4:10; 5:40)

Use the name of Jesus often, especially when you are praying for the sick and casting out demons. When the apostle Paul was casting out a spirit of fortunetelling, he spoke to the evil spirit saying 'in the name of Jesus Christ I command you to come out of her." The spirit obeyed. (Acts.16:18) We can use the name of Jesus when breaking something off of ourselves too. There is power in the name of Jesus.

EXERCISING OUR AUTHORITY IN CHRIST

CHAPTER FIVE

We live in a war zone, a place where the kingdom of God and the kingdom of darkness clash. As believers, we have been rescued out of the kingdom of darkness and placed into the kingdom of God's Son, Jesus Christ. (Col.1:13) The old kingdom is no longer to have any hold, control, influence or power over us. Because our enemy was defeated at the cross by the Son of God, we can be free in every area of our lives, including our health.

We are sons and daughters of the King of Kings. God is teaching us how to take dominion over our circumstances. In the Garden of Eden God gave man dominion. His instructions were to "Be fruitful and increase in number; fill the earth and subdue it. Rule over the fish of the sea and the birds of the air and over every living creature that moves on the ground." (Gen.1:28) Man was created to rule.

Luke 10:19 says that Jesus has given us "authority to trample on snakes and scorpions and to overcome all the power of the enemy", and He further stated that "nothing will harm us." We have been given the authority to overcome ALL the power of the enemy, but many of us can be using it more often than we do now.

Do we believe this kind of authority is real? Do we believe we can trample on the enemy and overcome him? Do we feel this is something we need to do in our lives frequently? Do we have a real enemy to contend with? Do we have an enemy who wants to harm us? An enemy who wants to harm me personally? My hope is that your answer to these questions is yes.

I ask these questions so that you will take a few minutes to think about what you believe about the reality of enemy activity against us, and our need to walk in authority. (I discuss the concept of enemy warfare in greater detail in my book "Ways of A Christian Warrior" if you are interested in knowing more about this subject.)

The concept of authority has many facets to it. My focus here will be primarily on the authority we have as believers regarding healing and deliverance. A simple definition of this kind of authority would be "the power and the right to heal the sick and set the captives free." In addition to having spiritual authority over sickness and darkness, we also have the Holy Spirit to help us and to endue us with power from on high.

Biblical Examples

Let's look at a few biblical examples to illustrate how Jesus used his authority to heal others. "When evening came, many who were demon possessed were brought to him (Jesus), and He drove out the spirits with a word and healed all the sick." (Mt. 8:16) Jesus spoke to a leper and said: "Be clean!" "Immediately the leprosy left him and he was cured." He raised Lazarus from death by praying and then speaking in a loud voice "Lazarus, come out!" (Mk.1:41,42) (Jn.11:43)

When Jesus encountered a woman who had been crippled by a spirit for 18 years He called to her and said "Woman, you are set free from your infirmity." Then He put his hands on her, and immediately she straightened up." When a man approached Jesus about his son who had seizures and suffered greatly. "Jesus **rebuked the demon**, and it came out of the boy, and he was healed from that moment." (Mt. 17:18) (LK.13:13,14)

Jesus used his authority to cast out demons and release healing. Jesus pronounced the leper clean and the crippled woman free. He commanded Lazarus to come out of his grave. He prayed but He also used his voice to command and to make pronouncements.

When Peter and John prayed for a crippled man, they commanded him to walk. (Acts 3:6) Peter used his authority and the power of the Lord to enable the man to walk. This man had been crippled from birth and with a few simple words of faith on the part of the apostles, the crippled man walked for the first time in his life.

Fight for Healing

When we enter God's kingdom through faith in Christ, this is the beginning of a wonderful new adventure with the Lord. God has plans and purposes for each one of us, and always wants the best for us. Jesus empowers believers so that we will participate with him in doing the works of the kingdom. Over the years I have observed that many believers seem to be waiting for an event to take place, i.e. waiting for God to heal them or do something else they have been asking for. And sometimes, patient waiting for the Lord to act is called for.

But recently I have come to realize that oftentimes God is waiting for us to act. He is waiting for you and I to exercise dominion over our circumstances. He has given us his power and his authority, and He wants us to use them to do something about our problems. He wants us to fight for what belongs to us. As we learn how to rule with God here on earth, we will be able to effect changes in our circumstances to a greater degree.

In Exodus 3 God told Moses that He was concerned about the suffering of the Israelites. They had been subjected to cruel and harsh treatment. Because the Lord was concerned about their wellbeing, He came down to "rescue them from the hand of the Egyptians and to bring them up out of that land into a good and spacious land, a land flowing with milk and honey." God's heart was to bring the Israelites into a beautiful place to live, and He assured them that He would drive out their enemies and help them take the land. (Ex. 34)

God rescued the Israelites from their bondage to the Egyptians and then He planned to bring his people into a new and beautiful land. To the Israelites this must have sounded so wonderful after their many years of hardship. They were going to a land filled with milk and honey, a land where God would be their God and they would be his chosen people. The day came when it was time to enter the land. God had prepared them for this day. When the people heard a report about giants living in this land, fear filled their hearts and they refused to fight with the

Lord for the new land. They grumbled and complained and wanted to return to their old land, to their old ways. (Numbers 13 & 14)

The point I want to make is this: God could have miraculously done something to prepare the land ahead of time so the Israelites wouldn't have had to fight for it. He performed many miracles on their behalf in order to set them free from Pharaoh's grasp. It would have been a really easy thing for God to drive out the inhabitants of the land before the Israelites got there. The point is that God didn't do this. He wanted his people to get involved in the battle. He prepared them for this, and He told them He would go before them and fight with them and for them and the land would be theirs. They had nothing to fear. The outcome had already been determined by God.

I find there are parallels for us today in this story of the Israelites and Moses. God rescues us from our bondage when we come to know Christ, and He brings us into his beautiful new kingdom. The Kingdom of God is a land filled with milk and honey, a land filled with the blessings of God. These blessings include good health. God could also heal us miraculously at any time, but oftentimes, like the Israelites, He wants us to take action to drive out the enemy, and take possession of our land, and He will help us. He has plans and purposes for us in doing this. It isn't to cause us harm, but rather to bless us and strengthen us, and to allow us to work together with him to possess the many blessings He has given us. Are we willing to fight for what is rightfully ours?

Believers take Authority

We fight by taking authority over the enemy and over all of his actions against us. We can do this in any area in which we feel we might be coming under enemy attack. Common areas of attack might be our health, finances, thought life, relationships with other people, our children, and so much more.

We have an enemy who is prowling around us like a roaring lion seeking to devour us. The good news is that we are not at the mercy of the enemy. We can do something to stop his activity and influence in our lives. As we learn to exercise our authority in Christ, we will no longer be the ones being overcome by the enemy or by our circumstances. We will be the victorious ones. We are more than conquerors through Christ who loves us. (Rom.8:37)

It is not always easy to know whether a sickness is just a sickness or whether the source of the illness is enemy activity. In recent years I've become more aware of how frequently the enemy attacks believers physically. Because of this, I now assume that a sickness or a pain is being caused by the enemy, and I take a stand against it. Learning to discern the presence of enemy activity is important. Once it is discerned, we are better able to take authority over the enemy and receive our healing.

How do we exercise our authority in the area of healing? Most often we will use the prayer of command. We command the sickness to leave and never return. We speak to the condition out loud and tell it to go. In essence, we are breaking the power of the enemy in our life or for someone else. We are breaking the control that sickness has over us. Sometimes we are to cancel the enemy's assignment against another. There are occasions when we will feel led to make a pronouncement regarding someone's healing or freedom. We might declare a healing into being.

We can exercise our authority with smaller afflictions as well as bigger ones. I've been learning to take authority over a lot of smaller things that try to afflict me. Whenever I feel a new ache in my body, or an illness of some kind just beginning, or any other new symptom that I haven't experienced before, I immediately take authority over it and tell it go.

We want to get rid of any aches, pain, or sickness as soon as we notice it, and before it can take root. Many of us will find it easier to be healed of new physical problems that occur, than getting free of afflictions that have been with us for a long time. Long-term illnesses will also respond to the prayer of command, it just takes many of us a little longer sometimes.

Scriptural Foundation

When I first began seeking after healing for myself personally, I wrote down many good scriptures on healing. I had faith for others to be healed but found it harder to believe for myself. Many of the scriptures came from the four gospels. I kept these verses all in one place and read them often during the day. I did this until I was convinced that God wanted to heal me.

Once I knew I had laid a good scriptural foundation, I could begin to use my authority to free myself from the illness. I knew that I was standing on solid ground. I used these scriptures and the prayer of command to free myself from the grip of the disease. I've been free for many years now, and am so grateful to the Lord for showing me that the root cause of the sickness was the enemy, and for helping me believe I could be set free from all sickness.

Helping Others be free from Demonic Oppression
Sometimes people know when they are under demonic oppression or influence of some kind. Not only can we be free from this, but we can also help others to gain their freedom. Before praying for a person in this situation, it would be good to do some preparation with the person beforehand. Take some time to chat together and try to find out why the person was afflicted. Was it because of sin, unforgiveness, a generational curse, involvement with the occult, etc. As we are speaking with the person, we are also using the gift of discernment. We are asking the Lord to show us what is going on. The Lord's heart is to see the person healed and set free, and He will help us discern the cause of the oppression.

Some kind of action will likely need to be taken such as: Leading a person into repentance and pronouncing the Lord's forgiveness for sins or actions. The person being prayed for may need to renounce prior sinful activities or may need to extend forgiveness to someone who caused them pain. In turn we can pray cleansing prayers over them. It's also a good idea for the person to submit every part of their lives to Christ, to his lordship. Basically, where the enemy once ruled them in a certain area, the person is choosing to ask Christ to rule over them instead of the enemy.

The person praying then can cut the person free in the name of Jesus. Or they can loose them from the enemy's hold by the blood of Jesus. Command the specific spirit, if known, to leave the person and never return. There may be more than one spirit, and that too will have to be addressed and cast out. Once the person has been set free, they might immediately receive their healing. If not, then pray for the person to be healed of their sickness. Pray for them to be healed from any negative effects that may have been caused in their bodies and their spirits. Pray blessings over the person. Ask the Holy Spirit to fill all those places where the enemy had been operating.

We can follow similar steps for ourselves too if we feel we need to be set free from something. For example, we might be suffering from an addiction of some kind, or we might feel some darkness oppressing us. We have the ability to release ourselves from the enemy's influence over us. We no longer have to suffer unnecessarily. Christ has made a way for us to overcome and enjoy freedom.

Complete Authority

When Jesus triumphed on the cross, He was given "all authority in heaven and on earth." All authority belongs to Christ and we belong to him. He is the source of our authority. He is also our role model. He commissioned us to go and do the same things He did. Because of this, we can exercise authority in the same areas Jesus did.

When Jesus walked the earth, He demonstrated his authority in numerous ways. When He calmed the wind and the waves, or rebuked storms, He was taking dominion over nature and breaking the power of what the enemy was trying to do to cause fear and harm to the disciples. He walked on water, and Peter was also able to walk on water for a short time. When the crowds were hungry and no food was available, Jesus multiplied food and fed thousands of people with baskets full of food leftover.

Jesus exercised authority over death when He raised Lazarus and others to life after they had died. He himself arose from the grave after three days and lives forever. Death could not hold him. And the power of death has been broken over us forever. Jesus defeated Satan and all his minions. He has won the war. The end has already been written, and Jesus is victorious. We are to be victorious with him. We can do all things through Christ.

HEALING FAITH

CHAPTER SIX

When it comes to healing, faith is an important ingredient. When faith is present, miracles happen. Each and every one of us has been given a measure of faith, but many of us don't understand how it works or how we can walk in it more effectively to overcome all the challenges we face in life.

Jesus often spoke about having faith for healing. When He encountered a woman with a bleeding problem, He told her that her faith had healed her, and she was healed from that moment. Another woman came to Jesus asking for prayer for her daughter. Jesus said "Woman, you have great faith. Your request is granted." A blind man came to Jesus and Jesus told him to "Go, your faith has healed you." Immediately he received his sight and followed Jesus. (Matt. 9:22; Matt.15:28; Mark 10:52)

I have spent many years reading numerous books by some of the great giants of the faith movement, and by people who operated in a powerful healing anointing. I wanted to have more faith for the healing of others and desired to see more breakthroughs in my own life in the area of physical healing.

As I understand it, the basic premise of the faith teaching is this: Ask God in faith for whatever it is you need, believe that you have received it and it will be yours. We also are to activate our faith by declaring what we believe out loud. It is based primarily on these two key scriptures:

"Have faith in God," Jesus answered. "I tell you the truth, if anyone says to this mountain, 'Go, throw yourself into the sea,' and does not doubt in his heart but believes that what he says will happen, it will be done for him. Therefore I tell you, whatever you ask for in prayer, believe that you have received it, and it will be yours." (Mark 11:22-24)

"But what does it say? "The word is near you; it is in your mouth and in your heart," that is, the word of faith we are proclaiming: That if you confess with your mouth, "Jesus is Lord," and believe in your heart that God raised him from the dead you will be saved. For it is with your heart that you believe and are justified, and it is with your mouth that you confess and are saved. " (Romans 10:8-10)

I learned so much from these writers, but somehow I couldn't always get it to work for me. I sometimes prevailed with smaller things like colds and pains, etc., but I wasn't able to overcome on a consistent basis. So, I put it all aside for a time.

Then in 2013, I went through a difficult period physically and I was desperate for answers. I began entreating the Lord about this and asking him to tell me what I was missing. Why couldn't I break through on some of these healings? What was the missing ingredient? Where was I going wrong? Why didn't I have enough faith?

During this time, the Lord gave me some spiritual insights and I was finally able to break through and receive healing. I want to share with you some of the wonderful truths relating to faith that the Lord revealed to me, so that you too will be able to experience more breakthroughs personally. Here are two important keys the Lord gave me to increase my faith: King Jesus invites us to ask him for things, and He tells us in advance that He will give us what we ask for. We will look at these two keys together in greater detail.

Jesus is the mightiest king who ever lived, and He lives today. He is the King of Kings and the Lord of Lords. We belong to him and we live in his kingdom. It is a glorious kingdom filled with good things. Our King loves us more than we can comprehend. We can approach the King's throne of grace anytime we want to, without fear, so that we may find help in our time of need. (Rev. 19:16; Heb. 4:16)

It is in the nature of kings to invite those in their kingdoms to petition them for things so that they can display their power and generosity in granting the request. We see this dynamic at work in two separate biblical stories.

King Xerxes. His story is found in the book of Esther. He was a mighty king who ruled over 127 provinces, including India. On four separate occasions, the king invites Queen Esther to make a request of him so that he could grant her request. He says to her "what is your petition? It will be given you. What is your request? Even up to half the kingdom, it will be granted." King Xerxes invites Esther to make a request, and before she even makes the request, he tells her that it will be granted. At that moment his integrity was on the line. According to the Bible, King Xerxes fulfilled Esther's requests.

King Herod. Herod lived during the time of Jesus and was one of the most evil kings in history. On his birthday he gave a banquet for a lot of important people. The daughter of Herodias came in and danced for him and for his guests. Herod was pleased with her so he said to her "ask me for anything you want and I'll give it to you. And he promised her with an oath 'whatever you ask I will give you, up to half my kingdom." That was a pretty risky thing for a king to do in front of so many people. Who knows what she might ask for that he would have to grant. The passage in Mark 6 says that "the king was distressed but because of his oaths and his dinner guests, he did not want to refuse her", so he did what she asked. He fulfilled her request even though he didn't want to.

Both of these unrighteous kings extended invitations to others to make requests of them. Both kings told the petitioners, before they made their requests, their petitions would be granted. And both kings followed through on their verbal commitments and did what was asked of them.

As believers, we belong to a righteous King, the Lord Jesus Christ. Our King Jesus has extended invitations to us to ask him for things so that He can fulfill our requests. These invitations are recorded for us in the gospels.

King Jesus invited us to "ask and it would be given to you." He also said: "And I will do whatever you ask in my name, so that the Son may bring glory to the Father. Another time Jesus said: You may ask me for anything in my name, and I will do it." And "Ask and you will receive, and your joy will be complete." (Mt.7:7; John 14:13; Jn.14:14: John 16:24: Matthew 7:11; Mt.7:8)

How many times have we all read these verses? Have we stopped to ponder their meaning? Jesus was very clear in his speech. "Ask me". "I will do it". "You will receive". It is King Jesus who is inviting you and me to ask him for whatever it is we are in need of. He is the mighty King who has the power and the authority to grant our requests and He desires to do this for us.

When the Lord made this connection for me, I could feel my faith levels rising and my thinking changed. I more clearly see Jesus as a mighty King inviting me to ask him for what I need, and when I ask I have an assurance that it will be done for me. I know it would be unthinkable for Jesus to say these words to us in the scriptures and then not fulfill his promises. I understood that not only would He grant our requests, but how much more our righteous King Jesus would do this for us, because He loves us so much.

We are positionally in an even better place than Queen

Esther was with King Xerxes. In a better place than Herodias's daughter was with King Herod. Both of them were invited to ask for up to half of the King's kingdom. We are sons and daughters of the King, members of his family, and have been given open access to our King and to everything that belongs to him.

No matter how many promises God has made, they are yes in Christ. God's answer to us is always yes. We can rely on the faithfulness and truthfulness of God. "But as surely as God is faithful, our message to you is not "Yes" and "No." For the Son of God, Jesus Christ, who was preached among you by me and Silas and Timothy, was not "Yes" and "No," but in him it has always been "Yes." For no matter how many promises God has made, they are "Yes" in Christ. And so through him the "Amen" is spoken by us to the glory of God." (2 Cor.1:18-20)

Additional Ways to increase our Faith
Spend time in the word of God. The word of God is our daily bread. We are to feed on every word that proceeds from the mouth of God. How else will we know what God's promises to us are? This is the main way God speaks to us. If we aren't hearing his voice much, spending more time in the scriptures will open the door for us. This will increase our ability to hear from the Lord almost immediately.

As we spend time in the word, we are spending time with the Word. Experiencing the presence of God close to us raises our faith levels, because we know He hears us.

The word of God is part of our armor, and I believe it to be one of the most important parts. The word of God is referred to as the sword of the spirit. (Eph.6:17) It is a double-edged sword that we can wield both offensively and defensively. We can use it to stand our ground when the enemy tries to attack us in a new way. And we can use the word of God to take back ground that the enemy has taken from us in the past. May the praise of God be in our mouths and a double-edged sword in our hands. (Ps. 149:6)

Choose to believe God and don't doubt. We are called believers, because that is what we do: we believe. We believe what the Bible says. We believe in the faithfulness and truthfulness of our loving heavenly Father. We believe He will do what He says He will do. We ask the Lord for something according to his word, we believe that his answer to us is yes, and then his power is released in our lives.

Our focus is on our mighty Savior, and on what He said He would do. We don't focus on what our eyes see, or on what we are feeling. We want to be ruthless about banishing all doubt and unbelief from our hearts and minds. During the midst of our difficulties, it can be easy for us to doubt God's good intentions for us. We can't always see the bigger picture the Lord is painting of our lives. Refuse to doubt God on any level. Stay focused on his goodness and on the promise you are contending for. Stay in a place of faith, not fear.

Add perseverance. I have learned to persevere until my

request comes to pass. When I am contending for a promise from God, I carry various scriptures in my heart and actively declare the verses out loud. I thank and praise the Lord out loud for all He is doing for me. I pray the scriptures back to the Lord. I actively work with the Lord to bring about the promise.

Don't give up if your answer doesn't come right away. Keep trusting God and persevering until your breakthrough comes. God is faithful and He won't let you down. Read the Parable of the Persistent Widow in Luke 18. Jesus spoke this parable to show his disciples that they should "always pray and not give up".

Did you know that the Lord perseveres with us too until his promises are fulfilled? Jacob was leaving his home to go to Haran to find a wife. He had a dream where he saw a stairway from earth to heaven and saw angels ascending and descending on it. Then he saw the Lord and the Lord said to him "I will not leave you until I have done what I have promised you." (Gen.28:15) The Lord's promises are so important to him that He will see them through to completion. So should we.

Always remember that our mighty King Jesus invites us to ask him for whatever we need. We know before we even ask, that God's answer to us is yes, it is always yes.

HEALING THROUGH NATURAL MEANS

CHAPTER SEVEN

There are times when God chooses to heal us through natural means. By that I mean He will reveal the cause of the sickness to us, and show us what steps we can follow in order to be healed. For example, we might be eating or drinking something that is making us ill, or wearing clothes or scents that we are allergic to, but don't realize it. In the case of an allergy the Lord would want us to know the cause of our discomfort, so that we could avoid that particular trigger, or even possibly be healed of the trigger so it no longer affects us in a negative way.

This is a very common way that the Lord uses to bring healing to us. The Lord heals us this way so that we can get to the root of the trouble, and prevent it from happening again, as well as prevent it from getting much worse. Once our eyes have been opened to this method of healing, we will begin to pay more attention to what the Lord may be showing us in the natural realm.

How do we receive healing through natural means? Most of these kinds of healings come through words of knowledge. As we seek the Lord for healing about something, a thought or an impression might drop into our minds about something we've been doing. We might have a knowing about something. Or the Lord might give us a dream. We want to be responsive to what the Lord is showing us. Why not try something you believe the Lord may be showing you? We have nothing to lose and everything to gain.

My doctor once put me on a medication that contained the vitamin Niacin. After I had been on this medication for about a month, I began having upset stomachs and passing what I think were gallstones. I started praying about this and asking the Lord why this was happening. I had an impression that it was because of the Niacin I was taking. I had not made the connection myself. I quit taking it immediately and within a few weeks my symptoms abated.

The Lord could prompt us to do something simple, like take a certain vitamin that our body is lacking. Don't dismiss this type of nudging from the Lord. You may have been asking him about some muscle soreness you were experiencing, and this is the way He answered you. Your muscle soreness and need for a certain vitamin were somehow connected and you didn't realize it, but the Lord did.

This actually happened to my sister. She was experiencing muscle soreness and her doctor told her that she needed more vitamin D. Her levels were very low. She began taking large doses of the vitamin and within a short time her muscle soreness stopped. So when my sister told me about this, I went to my doctor and asked him to check my vitamin levels. I found out I was even lower than my sister was. I believe the Lord used my sister to help me avoid problems I could have potentially faced.

Ask Two Questions

The Lord has healed me on numerous occasions through natural means. Any time something new or strange starts happening in my body, I pray and ask the Lord to show me the cause of it. I ask him why this is happening to me now. I work with the Lord to find if there is a natural cause that needs to be remedied.

I ask myself some questions too. Am I doing anything differently than I used to? Am I on any new medications? If yes, might this be a side effect of that? Have I added any new foods to my diet? Am I using any new creams for my body? Might I have injured a muscle recently and that's why I'm feeling this pain? Have I changed my laundry soap, etc? I ponder these things because I want my body to be healthy and I don't want to do anything that will prevent me from experiencing complete health.

Then I take the appropriate action. I do whatever the Lord might tell me to do. I don't just give in to it and let it take root. I also take authority over it right away and command the condition to go in the mighty name of Jesus.

Strange Rash Appeared

Some years ago, I began getting some round rash marks on my body that were the size of a 50 cent piece, about $1\frac{1}{2}$ inches in diameter. They were very strange looking and I had no idea what these were, so I went to the doctor. The doctor was a specialist in skin conditions and didn't know what this was either. She gave me some really good cream to use on the rash, and the rash began to go away. All during this time I was also asking the Lord to show me how I got this rash, and that is when I felt him impressing upon me to examine what new things I might have doing. The only new thing I could think of was that I was drinking a new fruit juice that had pineapple, orange juice and mango in it. I began drinking it, because I thought it would be healthy for my body to drink some fruit juice every day. As I thought about this juice, I remembered how I would get a few small canker sores in my mouth whenever I ate more than a few pieces of pineapple. So now I realized that it might have been the pineapple juice that was causing the problem.

I immediately quit drinking the juice and I never got the rash again. Had I not stopped to ask the Lord what caused the rash or had I not taken the time to think about what I was doing differently, I might have had to battle that rash for quite a while. Who knows what other problems it might have given me over time.

Hands started tingling

A while back, my hands started tingling, and my hands felt like they were going to sleep, especially at night. The tingling sensation was strong enough to wake me up. Again, I asked the Lord to show me what might be causing this. He reminded me that I had begun taking some new medication a few weeks prior to this. So I wondered if this could be the cause of the tingling.

I noticed some time earlier that when I took a generic drug I experienced some odd side effects. At the time I thought I might be allergic to the antibiotic I was taking. When this tingling happened, I checked the medication, and found that I was taking the generic form of the drug, and wondered if this was the cause of my tingling hands. I quit taking the generic medication and switched over to the brand name and within a couple of days my symptoms were gone, no more tingling in my hands.

Headache Cure

Some years ago when our son was young and we were living in England, we took a trip to visit Brad's family in California. I began experiencing a really bad headache. I had never had such a bad headache before; in fact I hardly ever have a headache. This one alarmed me. After about 24 hours of this terrible pain, I was seriously thinking that I needed to go to the Emergency Room of the local hospital.

Before I did, I thought I would pray about it and ask the Lord to help me. I felt He showed me that the cause of my headache was the new sunglasses I had been wearing. The sun was very bright when we first arrived in California, so I had purchased an inexpensive pair of sunglasses to protect my eyes. I was wearing them a lot, because I wasn't used to the brightness of the sun in California.

I had never heard of such a thing, that a severe headache could be caused by wearing sunglasses. I was desperate to try anything, so I quit wearing them, and by the next day my headache was completely gone. I never wore those glasses again. Only the Lord could have made the connection between a pair of sunglasses and a very painful headache. A short while later I began to realize that I should have asked the Lord about the cause of my headache when the headache first began. I could have saved myself a lot of pain and discomfort. Now I know to do this right away when I feel pain in my body, and after reading this chapter you will too.

The sooner we can discern the cause of our affliction, the sooner we can be healed from it and keep it from happening again and again. This doesn't work with every condition, but you will be surprised how often it does work and how simple a solution it is.

Painful Recurring Sore Throats

Sometimes we have conditions that continue to reoccur with some frequency. When this happens, with the Lord's help, we can often figure out the cause of these recurring conditions and eliminate them from our lives forever.

Some years ago I had a series of painful sore throats. These sore throats afflicted me every six months, and each time they were bad enough that I was prescribed antibiotics for it. I was concerned about the effect of taking antibiotics so often, and that drove me to begin asking the Lord why this kept happening. The answer came the next time I began experiencing yet another sore throat.

An impression came to me that I should look into my mouth and my throat. Somehow I had not thought to do that before. I got out my flashlight and started looking at the spot that was causing me pain. As I looked closely

I could see what looked like food stuck there in a crevice inside my mouth, in the back on the right. I believe it was in a part of my tonsils.

Then I felt like I should try to remove what I was seeing. So I got a Qtip, a little stick that has a small cotton ball on the end of it. I wet it and used it to dislodge that piece of food. Because it was so far back in my mouth it wasn't easy to get it out, but I stayed with it until it was gone. Then I gargled with some warm salt water a few times.

Amazingly my throat felt much better instantly. After that time I had a couple of small sore throats beginning and I handled them in the same way. Because of this, they never developed into a major painful throat infection. And within a short time, I never suffered from that kind of a sore throat again. It was such a wonderful feeling and I was so grateful that the Lord showed me the cause and helped me to be free of these.

So, when we next have a pain or illness beginning in our body, rebuke it, and also ask the Lord to show us why this is happening, and especially so when this is a recurring affliction of some kind. And then take the necessary action required.

King Hezekiah
God used natural means to heal King Hezekiah. Hezekiah was at the point of death and he prayed and wept before the Lord. The word of the Lord came to the prophet Isaiah for Hezekiah: "This is what the LORD, the God of

your father David, says: I have heard your prayer and seen your tears; I will heal you. On the third day from now you will go up to the temple of the LORD. [6] I will add fifteen years to your life."............[7] Then Isaiah said, "Prepare a poultice of figs." They did so and applied it to the boil, and he recovered. (2 Kings 20)

God said He would heal King Hezekiah, and that Hezekiah would be well enough to go up to the temple of the Lord in three days. I find it intriguing that the Lord didn't supernaturally heal him instantly, although He did supernaturally add 15 years to his life span and hastened his physical healing process. Instead Hezekiah was told to apply a poultice of figs to his wound. The natural was working together with the supernatural. A prophetic word was given plus a poultice was applied.

Listen to the Lord's Voice
The Lord is continually speaking to us and trying to help us in so many ways. But I wonder how often we ignore that quiet inner prompting we get sometimes? For example, we may feel a prompting not to eat or drink something. Because we aren't positive it is the Lord warning us, we sometimes go ahead and do it. And sickness might be the result.

A couple of years ago I was in India, sitting at a table with others and I started to eat a shrimp. It looked delicious. But when I put it up to my nose, it didn't smell right and I felt that I shouldn't eat it. I warned the others at my table about this. One person had a shrimp in her mouth and immediately spit it out. Two others went ahead and ate the shrimp and got very sick for 2 days. That sickness could have been avoided.

If we want to experience more of these types of healings through natural means, we will want to attune our ear to the Holy Spirit and to what He might be saying to us. Just because a thing is good, doesn't mean it is good for each one of us. We are uniquely different, and something that might affect me negatively might not affect you. And vice versa. The Lord is the one who knows us best, and He will help us because He loves us so very much.

In summary, ask the Lord to show you the cause of your pain or sickness. Listen carefully to what He might be showing you, as it often comes like a fleeting thought. Don't ignore the impression because it seems too simple or seems like it couldn't be the cause. Then take the appropriate action. You will be glad that you did.

POWER OF PRAISE

CHAPTER EIGHT

When we first began working with the ministry in India, I came down with pneumonia and was very weakened by it physically. I was coughing non stop and was not able to sleep very much because of the coughing. In addition, when I was able to sleep, I was having a lot of bad dreams about snakes attacking me. I was going through a physical attack as well as a spiritual attack. I was so weakened from it, that I found it difficult to pray or try to stand in faith, so I asked some close friends to pray for me.

In my weakness, I had a thought that I should play a certain worship CD I had purchased but had not yet listened to. As the music played, I started to worship with it, and something interesting happened. I began feeling stronger on the inside. It was as if my spirit had connected with the Holy Spirit. I began singing at the top of my lungs and I felt a release of power coming forth through that. It's a little hard to explain, but I knew that I had broken through the darkness of what I was going through.

Then, that night as I was sleeping, I had a dream about honey. There was a large amount of honey positioned directly above me. In the dream I heard the sound of a lever, and then the honey was released and poured down all over me. I was covered in it. The next morning I began to feel better physically and felt a little stronger. It took some months before I was completely restored, but my healing was released through worship that day. It was a wonderful new revelation for me about the power of praise. Praise set this captive free from the enemy's strong attack against me.

The power of praise is particularly effective when we come under enemy attack in some way. There is a wonderful scripture on praise that I have often heard quoted from Psalm 8:2 "From the lips of children and infants you have ordained praise." One day the Lord highlighted the second part of that verse to me, which is "because of your enemies, to silence the foe and the avenger." The Lord ordained praise for us because of our enemies, to silence our foes. Isn't that interesting? Praise has power to defeat enemy activity in our lives. When we spend time praising God, this creates an atmosphere of God's presence around us. This causes the enemy to flee from us.

Some time after I was completely healed, I began to search the scriptures to see if anything like this had happened in the Bible. I found some great stories of deliverance from enemy activity through the power of praise.

Paul & Silas in Prison Their story is found in Acts 16. Paul and Silas had been severely flogged, thrown into prison and their feet put into stocks. About midnight Paul and Silas were "praying and singing hymns to God." What an amazing response considering what had just happened to them. Look at what happens next. "The other prisoners were listening to them. Suddenly there was such a violent earthquake that the foundations of the prison were shaken. At once all the prison doors flew open, and everybody's chains came loose."

A mighty demonstration of the power of God was released into the prison. All the inmates plus the man in charge of the prisoners (the jailer) experienced this supernatural event. As a result, the jailer and his whole household were saved, and Paul and Silas were given favor with him. The very next day Paul and Silas were set free from prison.

Battle of Jericho The story of the battle of Jericho is found in Joshua 6. The Lord announces that He has delivered the city of Jericho into the hands of the Israelites. Then the Lord gives them instructions on what they should do. The instructions included having 7 priests blowing their trumpets (ram's horns) with the ark of the Lord accompanying them all. The priests blew the trumpets while they marched around the city. And the Lord's presence accompanied them.

"When Joshua had spoken to the people, the seven priests carrying the seven trumpets before the LORD went forward, blowing their trumpets, and the ark of the LORD's covenant followed them. The armed guard marched ahead of the priests who blew the trumpets, and the rear guard followed the ark. All this time the trumpets were sounding." (Joshua 6:8,9) They did this for seven days. On the seventh day, the walls of the city collapsed and the Israelites conquered the city. The Lord helped them in battle against their enemies.

I love what the Lord says in Numbers 10:9: "When you go into battle in your own land against an enemy who is oppressing you, sound a blast on the trumpets. Then you will be remembered by the LORD your God and rescued from your enemies." We don't blow Shofars, i.e. ram's horns or trumpets, very much in our churches, but we do spend time worshipping the Lord. When we are worshipping the Lord, He will remember us and rescue us from our enemies.

Jehoshaphat in battle Another battle story. You may be wondering why battle stories are relevant to healing. When we are in need of healing we often find ourselves in a battle with the forces of darkness. Spiritual battles are to be fought with spiritual weapons, and praise is one of the most important weapons we have at our disposal when we are in the midst of a spiritual battle.

2 Chronicles 20 describes the story of King Jehoshaphat. He and Israel had come under attack by their enemies. The Lord encouraged them: "Do not be afraid or discouraged because of this vast army. For the battle is not yours but God's." The Lord gave the King additional instructions on what he and the people were to do, and assured them that He would be with them in the battle and He would deliver them. The King and all the people of Judah and Jerusalem were so encouraged and grateful for what the Lord was going to do for them, that they all fell down in worship before the Lord. Some Levites also

stood up and praised the LORD, the God of Israel, with very loud voices.

The next morning Jehoshaphat appointed men to sing to the Lord and to praise him for the splendor of his holiness as they went out to war. As they began to sing and praise the Lord, the Lord set ambushes against their enemies, and their enemies began destroying one another. When the army of Judah arrived, they saw only dead bodies. God had fought the battle for them while they worshipped and praised him. The plunder was so great that it took the Israelites three days to collect it all.

MODERN DAY STORIES

Here are some modern day stories of breakthroughs that others experienced as a direct result of worshipping and praising God. May you be encouraged that God still does miracles, and that praise and worship can play a role in this.

Kenneth E. Hagin He was a pioneer in the faith movement for a long time and helped many of us learn more about what it means to have faith for healing and other things. When he was a teenager, he was bedridden with severe heart problems and an incurable blood disease. His doctors told him that he was dying. There was nothing more that medicine could do to help him. During this time, he became a Christian and he started reading his Bible. God began highlighting Mark 11:22-24 to him. This passage says "I tell you, whatever you ask for in prayer, believe that you have received it, and it will be yours." It also says if we don't doubt, but believe that

81

what we say will happen, it will be done for us. Mr. Hagin began believing this scripture with all his heart and in a short period of time he was completely healed.

Usually his story stopped here, but I read in one of his books a while back that he realized that his healing was released after he began praising God for it. If I am remembering the story correctly, it was when he was praising God that he knew without a doubt that the scripture in Mark was true and that he was healed, and that caused him to praise God even more. Then he exercised his faith and began to stand up, even though that had been physically impossible for him to do. Faith plus worship brought about the healing he was seeking.

One time Mr. Hagin told a story of a woman missionary who had been healed of smallpox a long time ago. As the woman was praying for her healing she had a vision, and in the vision she saw a set of scales. One side was marked "Prayer" and the other side was marked "Praise". She could see that the side marked prayer was very weighty while the side marked praise was almost empty. Then she felt the Lord telling her that she would be healed when the amount of praise on the scales reached the amount of prayer. So she began praising God continually and within a short time she was completely healed. What a great combination, prayer and praise together.

Sophal in Prison. Sophal is the leader of a movement in a country in Southeast Asia. He is an amazing man who has faced many trials and dangers during his lifetime. I've heard him tell this story on several occasions. There was a period of time in his country when many Christians and others were being killed by the regime in charge. Sophal was able to survive this terrible time; the worst seemed to be over and churches there were being revived. Suddenly, without warning, Sophal was arrested. He was tortured for 70 days. He was in great pain, his health was failing and he was feeling really weak and very low. He began worshipping God.

The song he sang was this:
"I've got a river of life flowing out of me.
Makes the lame to walk and the blind to see.
Opens prison doors, sets the captives free,
I've got a river of life flowing out of me."
(Song written by L. Casebolt)

The prisoner in the cell next to him asked him how he could be worshipping God when he had been sent here to die. The prisoner who asked this was a general in the army and Sophal led him to Christ. The general was executed three days after this encounter. As Sophal continued to sing and worship the Lord, many others in the prison began singing with him and many came to know Christ.

One day as he was worshipping, heaven opened and Sophal saw many angels in heaven. The angels were all singing the same song with him, in his own language. One of the angels told Sophal to fast, to eat nothing. He was already slowing starving to death because he and the other prisoners were only given one small bowl of rice each day. Sophal obeyed the angel and refused the meager portions of food he was offered. The jailers were worried that he would die, so they began offering him larger amounts of good food to tempt him into eating. He kept refusing to eat, and became so weak that he was sent to the hospital to die.

A doctor at the prison hospital recognized that Sophal was a Christian and knew he had done nothing wrong to deserve being imprisoned. So the doctor decided to try to help Sophal escape. He told Sophal he would leave the door unlocked that night and that Sophal should try to escape. He didn't have much time left. That night there was a huge storm, with lots of thunder and lightning. The lightning hit the prison building and caused all the power and lights to go off. Sophal knew that God must have brought this storm to help him, so as he lay there in the darkness, he gathered up his courage and what little strength he had left. He was so weak he couldn't walk. He crawled out the door right past the guard and down some steps. Miraculously the guard didn't see him crawling by. Somehow he managed to get outside, and the doctor was waiting for him in his car. He was free.

Praise is a Powerful Weapon

Never underestimate the power that praise can release in our lives. "May the praise of God be in their mouths (the saints) and a double edged sword in their hands." (Psalm 149:6) Isn't this a great picture? We are to be armed for battle and part of our preparedness is that the praise of God be in our mouths. We praise God for who He is. We thank him for all He has done for us and all He is going to do for us. We worship him because He is worthy of all praise and adoration. We worship him because we love him. And in the process of this, his presence draws near to us and his power is released on our behalf. The next time you need a breakthrough in healing or something else, add big doses of praise and worship to your prayers.

THE STRANGE AND THE UNUSUAL

CHAPTER NINE

The Bible contains some strange and unusual healing stories. I will be sharing some of these stories, and others from recent times, because I want to shake up our thinking about what God can do and what He might do. The best way to approach this is for us to look at some of the things He has already done. God is the Creator of all things. He is the author of the new. God's ways with us are so unique at times. He does things that have never been done before. Why wouldn't He do this with us if He felt it was needed for some reason unknown to us?

We have a tendency to put God in a box that we are comfortable with. Reading the Bible shows us that God doesn't fit into any box of our preconceived ideas and He never will. One phrase I used to hear a lot in Christian circles is that God is a gentleman and that He wouldn't do anything we weren't comfortable with. Not true.

I've had various times in my 38 years with the Lord where I have had to make an adjustment in my thinking or learn something new that was challenging to me in some way. I've been in meetings where the Holy Spirit is moving and some very strange things begin to happen. Strange things such as: people feeling the presence of God like a heaviness on their body and laying down on the floor, or standing still like statues unable to move for long periods of time as God healed them of something.

I've seen people roaring like a lion, as they were being empowered to fight the enemy.

I once saw a man's body moving like a jackhammer. He was bending forward and backward for hours. I asked him later what God was doing with him and he told me he was being healed from some emotional pain from childhood. The first time I saw people 'drunk in the spirit' I found it a little hard to watch. It wasn't until I experienced this myself that I realized how wonderful and healing an experience it could be.

Why do many people shake under the power of God? Or why do some start running around the sanctuary? Why does laughter break out at times when it almost seems disrespectful to others in the meeting? When the Spirit is moving, sometimes the fire of God will fall on believers. They start burning up with heat. Why does God sometimes release oil through people's hands as they are praying for the sick to be healed? Why does God put gold teeth into people's mouths? I've seen what looked like golden rain falling in a meeting. I've had gold flecks on my face and hands. So many strange things, could they really be from God? I believe the answer is often yes.

The reality is that God sometimes works in ways we don't expect. Over the years I've seen hundreds of strange things, sometimes God and sometimes not. I've learned how to be comfortable when God's Holy Spirit moves in unexpected ways. We want to remain open to the Holy Spirit and choose not to be offended by what we see or experience. Trust that God knows what He is doing.

Jesus was often shaking up his disciples through his words and his actions. He was frequently taking them out of their comfort zones, and I believe He might wish to do the same with us. He doesn't want his children stuck in some kind of liturgical box of tradition. Let's allow the Holy Spirit to help us get rid of any preconceived ideas we might have picked up as to how God works and how He might choose to heal us or heal others. Let's look at a few unusual biblical healings.

Moses and a snake: In Numbers 21 the Israelites were grumbling and complaining against the Lord just after the Lord helped them win a battle. They were complaining about the way the Lord was providing for them. The Lord sent venomous snakes into their midst. The people realized they sinned by speaking against the Lord and they asked Moses to pray that the Lord would remove the snakes. Moses prayed for the people.

The Lord responded by telling Moses to make a snake and put it up on a pole, so that anyone who was bitten by a venomous snake could look at the snake on the pole and live. Moses obeyed the Lord and made a bronze snake and put it up on a pole. Whenever someone was bitten by a snake, he or she would look at the bronze snake Moses made and live. He wouldn't die from the snake's venom.

The Israelites could be healed of a snake bite by looking at a bronze snake on a pole. Pretty unusual right? They didn't even have to pray. All they had to do was to look at the snake Moses made. I find it interesting that God didn't remove the snakes from the Israelites as they desired. He allowed the snakes to remain, but gave them a way to be healed. The people soon moved on from that place, so it's likely they didn't have to worry about the snakes for too much longer.

Jesus healed 2 Blind Men. The first story is found in John 9, the healing of a man who was born blind. "Jesus spit on the ground, made some mud with the saliva, and put it on the man's eyes. "Go," he told him, "wash in the Pool of Siloam". The man did as Jesus said and he "came home seeing".

In another similar story of a blind man being healed, Jesus put spit on the man's eyes and then laid hands on his eyes. This story is found in Mark 8. Jesus prays for the man twice and the man's eyes were opened and he saw everything clearly.

Jesus used his spit on two occasions to heal blind men. This would be a really odd thing for us to do today, wouldn't it? If we saw someone doing it, it would be very off-putting. A person's saliva can hold some very bad germs that could cause someone to get very sick. If we were to do this without the leading of the Holy Spirit, it could have some adverse consequences.

Jesus Heals a Demon Possessed Man. The story is found in Mark 5. A man was possessed by a legion of demons. His affliction was so bad that he was confined to live in the tombs by himself. He was often chained hand and foot by people trying to subdue him. Day and night he would cry out and cut himself with stones. Most people would have been afraid of him, but Jesus was different.

Jesus confronts the demons in the man and issues the command for them to "Come out of this man!" The demons begged Jesus to let them go into a herd of pigs feeding nearby on a hillside. Jesus gave them permission and they left the man and went into the herd of pigs. The man was fully restored, and was soon reconciled with his family. Meanwhile, once the demons went into this huge herd of about 2,000 pigs, the pigs rushed down a steep hillside and into the lake. The entire herd drowned. Such was the effect of the demons on that herd. It makes one marvel all the more that that poor, afflicted, demon-possessed man was able to survive such a strong possession by the enemy. How beautiful the compassion of God was for this one suffering man.

Today, if something like this were to happen, we would most likely be sued by the owner of the pigs for the lost herd. That makes it imperative that we know we are following God if we ever feel led to do something out of the ordinary.

Follow the Leading of the Holy Spirit
We want to follow the leading of the Holy Spirit every time we pray for the sick. Jesus often said that He could only do what He sees his Father doing. It is my belief that the Father told him to pray for the blind men in that particular way, and Jesus did it as an act of obedience.

This should be a principle we follow when we pray for the

sick. We listen to the voice of the Holy Spirit and follow what the Spirit is telling us to do. If we feel the Holy Spirit is leading us to do something very strange, we will want to pray, and make sure that we are hearing his voice, and not a counterfeit voice of the enemy. If we are in doubt about it, it's better not to do something that might inadvertently harm someone.

There are a lot of things done in the name of the Lord that are not from the Lord and this has caused some damage in the body of Christ. I recently heard a story in the news of an exorcism gone wrong. People were trying to deliver a young woman from some demons and somehow caused her death. They may have been well intentioned, but it is never ok to harm anyone physically in healing or deliverance. Everything we do must be undergirded in the love of God for the person.

I've seen and heard a lot of crazy things when it comes to deliverance ministry. Some people yell and shout at the demons to leave. Some ministers will wave their arms around while they are shouting. Some try to get people to throw up their demons or cough them out. Some are overly rough and mean to the person they are ministering to. Others taunt the demons unnecessarily or engage a demon in conversation. Some ministers actually charge money for delivering people. This should not be.

Casting Out Demons
In general when one is casting out demons strange things often occur. Situations can arise that might make one a little fearful. When we are doing conferences in India we

often have power encounters. The presence of the Holy Spirit will be so strong that demons will make their presence known in a person who is attending the conference. The person might begin shrieking, or writhing on the floor like a snake. One can often see it in the eyes of an afflicted person who will look at you with intense hatred or fear.

When my husband Brad and I lived in England we often found ourselves in a deliverance type of situation unexpectedly. We would be praying for someone about a simple problem, when suddenly a demon would manifest itself. When this happened we often felt uncomfortable, but over time God was gracious to us and helped us know what to do. Every situation was different, so we had to learn how to flow with the Holy Spirit in order for the person to be set free.

One time I was praying for a dear friend of mine and had a word of knowledge about her grandmother. As I began praying about my friend's grandmother, suddenly my friend jumped up and ran out of the house and into the bushes across the street and acted like a wild animal. Scary yes. Unusual definitely.

Another time I was praying for someone in our home group, because she was hurting over something. Suddenly she said she felt hands on her throat and said she was being strangled. She was having trouble breathing. We had to do something quickly to get that demonic spirit off of her.

In both of these situations, my friends were set free and were beautifully healed by the Lord. Let the Holy Spirit be your guide and always minister with love. The Lord will help you in every ministry type of situation you find yourself in. We don't need to fear the strange and the unusual.

We will look now at some stories of modern day healers who did some unusual things in their ministries. I share these stories because God used these two men in unusual ways to bring about healing and deliverance for thousands of people. I am not advocating that we imitate these techniques. I just want you to be aware that God uses different methods to heal people. These stories can be found on the internet.

William Branham's Healing Gift. I have been reading about the life of William Branham a lot in recent years. Branham was an amazing man of faith that God used to bring many people to Christ and to heal multitudes during the 1940's and 1950's. When his healing gift first began, this is how the gift operated: He was told by an angel that when he prays for a sick person, he was to hold the person's right hand with his left hand. Then he was to stand quietly. Demon-caused diseases would have a physical effect on his body. His hand would swell up and other things would show on his hand like red dots.

Then WB would pray for the person. He was told by the angel, that if the swelling leaves his left hand, the disease has left the person, and he was to pronounce the person healed. If the swelling didn't leave his hand, he was to pray a blessing over the person and walk away. WB had been given a unique gift and a great many people were healed through this gift. You have to admit that out of all the ways God might choose to heal someone, this way was unusual.

Smith Wigglesworth. Smith Wigglesworth was a well-known evangelist/healer who lived during the latter part of the 1800's and died in 1947. When one hears some of the stories from his ministry, you know you are hearing strange and unusual things, but also hearing about the healing power of God moving through this man. SW raised 23 people from the dead.

SW was praying for a man with no feet, when he felt led to tell the man to go and buy himself some new shoes. In obedience, the man went to the shoe store, but of course the clerk thought he was a bit nutty for wanting to buy shoes when he had no feet. After some discussion, the clerk brought him two new shoes. When the man put his leg into the first shoe, a miraculous thing happened. He grew a foot that filled the shoe. The same thing happened with his other leg. As he put his leg into the second shoe, another new foot miraculously grew to fit into the shoe. Can you imagine the awe and wonder of that miracle of God?

SW has punched persons in the stomach with such force that they moved part way across a room. This was in order to heal them of a stomach affliction of some kind. When he did this, the people were healed and suffered no other ill effects from the punch. When people questioned him on this technique he would reply that he wasn't hitting the person, he was hitting the devil.

Hearing stories of people being punched in the stomach causes me a little discomfort because love does no harm to its neighbor, and if someone was hurt physically by SW's actions, that would not be ok. It is said that he sometimes would hit or slap a place on a person's body where the demon was. It's hard to assess something like this when one is reading an account of what happened rather than seeing it with one's own eyes. This had to have taken place at the leading of the Holy Spirit or the people wouldn't have all been healed, and some of them might have gotten hurt. Always remember to follow the leading of the Holy Spirit every time you pray for someone else. And always follow the way of love and all will be well.

Transportation

Did you know that sometimes God supernaturally transports people to have them pray for others? Sometimes this is done in our spiritual bodies but it can also occur with our physical bodies. In Acts 8, an angel of the Lord led Philip to go to a Eunuch, and he explained to the man about Jesus. Then the eunuch was baptized. As soon as this happened "the Spirit of the Lord suddenly took Philip away". Philip was transported to another location.

I heard one well known prophetic man tell a story where someone was transported to pray for him. He was traveling overseas, when he started suffering from

96

severe stomach pains. The next day he was supposed to be speaking at a conference. That night a person appeared suddenly in his hotel room to pray for him and the prophetic man was instantly healed. The person then disappeared.

There was a group of intercessors led by Francis Metcalfe during the 1950's and 60's. She and this group prayed so fervently that God opened up a portal of some kind in one of their homes, and periodically some of the ladies would be transported somewhere by the Holy Spirit to pray for others.

I have experienced this type of healing prayer. Years ago I had a dream where I was transported to a foreign country to pray for the healing of an elderly woman. I felt like I was in Holland in a small town. As I prayed the woman was healed. Was this a real spiritual experience or just a dream? To me it felt like my spirit actually went to that country and prayed for that woman as my body slept in my bed.

IN CONCLUSION

Healing Includes Salvation, Physical and Emotional Healing. God's plan included healing that would encompass the whole person, not just renewing our spirits through the gift of salvation or healing for our bodies. His plan also includes healing for our soul area, for our emotions. If you think about it, doesn't it make sense that the Lord would want to heal every part of us? All of our parts are interconnected, with each part affecting the other. What kind of love would that be, to leave part of us in emotional and physical pain, and not heal the rest? Why would God renew our spirits and not our bodies too? God isn't like that. He is love and is the embodiment of love.

Over the years God has brought me so much healing both physically and emotionally. After the death of my dear Father in 1990, God revealed himself to me as my heavenly Father. He poured his unconditional love into my heart and healed many of the hurts I had experienced over the years. For six months I would cry deeply, and not even know why I was crying. And afterwards, I always felt so much lighter and freer, and experienced so much more of the presence of my heavenly Father within me. This kind of emotional healing is very real and very powerful in the life of a believer.

We have been given the Keys to the Kingdom. God has given us everything we need to walk in healing. We have been given the keys of the kingdom. "I will give you the keys of the kingdom of heaven; whatever you bind on earth will be bound in heaven; and whatever you loose on

99

earth will be loosed in heaven." (Matt. 16:19)

We have the ability to bind and to loose. This means we can bind the enemy's activity against ourselves and others, and we can loose the blessings of heaven here on earth, and the work will be done in heaven. "Do not be afraid little flock, for your Father has been pleased to give you the kingdom." (Luke 12:32) The Kingdom with all its authority and blessings belongs to us. We are the Lord's 'little flock'.

There is so much we don't know about the spiritual realm or the ways of God. God will use anyone or anything to heal his beloved. Always remember that He is the Lord who heals us, the Lord who wants to heal us. And He uses a variety of methods to do this. When it comes to healing never give up on him. Healing will be yours.